FATE'S KITE

OTHER BOOKS BY DAVE SMITH

POETRY

Night Pleasures: New and Selected Poems (1992)
Cuba Night (1990)
The Roundhouse Voices: Selected and New Poems (1985)
Gray Soldiers (1984)
In the House of the Judge (1983)
Homage to Edgar Allan Poe (1981)
Dream Flights (1981)
Blue Spruce (1981)
Goshawk, Antelope (1979)
Cumberland Station (1977)
In Dark, Sudden with Light (1977)
Drunks (1975)
The Fisherman's Whore (1974, 1993)
Mean Rufus Throw Down (1973)
Bull Island (1970)

FICTION

Southern Delights (1984)
Onliness (1981)

CRITICISM

The Essential Poe (1991)
Local Assays: On Contemporary American Poetry (1985)
The Pure Clear Word: Essays on the Poetry of James Wright (1982)

ANTHOLOGIES

New Viriginia Review 8 (1991)
New Viriginia Review 4 (1986)
The Morrow Anthology of Younger American Poets (1985)

FATE'S KITE

POEMS, 1991-1995

DAVE SMITH

LOUISIANA STATE UNIVERSITY PRESS

BATON ROUGE AND LONDON

1995

To Phoebe,

In continuous friendship and in the pleasure of her company, whether in words or person.

Dave Smith
July 12, 1998

Copyright © 1991, 1994, 1995 by Dave Smith
All rights reserved
Manufactured in the United States of America
First printing
04 03 02 01 00 99 98 97 96 95   5 4 3 2 1

Designer: Amanda McDonald Key
Typeface: Bembo
Typesetter: Impressions, a division of Edwards Brothers
Printer and binder: Thomson-Shore, Inc.

The author wishes to thank the editors of the following journals, especially Hilda Raz, for first publishing these poems, sometimes revised: *American Poetry Review:* "Watering the Dog," "Train to St. Andrews, Scotland," "Performing Fiction"; *Denver Quarterly:* "Cows Calling," "The Righteousness of Farrakhan," "Breasts," "Fiddlers," "Accounts"; *Double Take:* "Making a Statement"; *Georgia Review:* "Burglar Alarm"; *Kenyon Review:* "Arising," "Nine Ball," "Quail," "Field Dressing," "Fantastic Pelicans Arrive," "Descending"; *New Orleans Review:* "First Tournament Learning Experience," "Gold Bird and the Age," "A Lay of Spring"; *New Virginia Review:* "Home Prayer," "The Franklin Street Quadrilles"; *Partisan Review:* "Crying in the Streets," "A Map of Your Small Town"; *Poetry at the End of the Century:* "A Tune for Maura Dooley" (as "A Change of Tune"); *Poetry Ireland:* "Mississippi River Bridge," "Ghost Houses," "Green Duty," "Old Country"; *Prairie Schooner:* "One Hundred Twenty-Nine Dollars," "Brittany," "Velvet Running," "Wolves," "Lunch" (as "Power Lunch"), "Palm Trees at 1430 Knollwood Drive"; *Southern Humanities Review:* "Doctor's Office"; *Southern Indiana Review:* "Circa 1650," "Fireflies at Bennington, July 4," "Answer to a Poet's Last Letter," "The Gods in My Belly Listen"; *Southern Review:* "Elegy for My Friend's Suit," "Stalled on the Ebb Tide"; *Southwest Review:* "In the Nansemond River," "Wreck in the Woods"; *Spoon River Review:* "Seafarer," "The Innerness of Churchland," "Compost Pile," "Hammer and Sickle," "Elizabeth River Water Skiers," "On His Son's New Blue Guitar"; *Triquarterly:* "Louis Armstrong & the Astronauts Meet at the Langley AFB Pool," "A Supernatural Narrative," "A Librarian's Gift," "Nature Moment," "Another Nature Moment," "Mississippi River Bridge," "About the Farmer's Daughter," "Irish Whiskey in the Backyard"; *Virginia Quarterly Review:* "Canary Weather in Virginia," "The Bullpasture and the Cowpasture Couple," "Latin Lesson."

"The Louisiana Sea of Faith," "Almost at Sea," and "Water Pitcher" first appeared in *The Writer's Path: An Anthology.*

"Boys in the Square at Bologna" and "Wreckage at Lake Pontchartrain" first appeared in the *New Yorker.*

Library of Congress Cataloging-in-Publication Data

Smith, Dave, 1942–
    Fate's kite: poems, 1991–1995 / Dave Smith.
        p.   cm.
    ISBN 0-8071-2040-5 (alk. paper). — ISBN 0-8071-2041-3 (pbk. :
alk. paper)
    I. Title.
PS3569.M5173F38   1995
811'.54—dc20   95-24788
                                                                                   CIP

The paper in this book meets the guidelines for permanance and durability of the Committee on Production Guidelines for Book Longevity of the Council on Library Resources. ♾

This book is dedicated to
C. Edward Russell, Jr.

. . . soe they continue sometymes burninge and sometymes scarpinge, vntill the boate haue sufficient bothowmes.

—Thomas Hariot, "Making the Log Canoe"

Cruising and playing the radio
With No Particular Place to Go

—Chuck Berry

CONTENTS

I

III

IV

I

ARISING

Did he peek like a child where nippled sunlight poured,
did he call from cradling dark a woman to come,
did he brush off gravel, aware of himself,
did he sing in skull's studio as men now do,
did he first unfill what swelled his lower parts,
did he hear that water blooming like her breath,
did he know which way up held his face, his feet,
did he fit his palms where the rock must answer,
did he fight the alum of hunger's first bite,
did he smell what the rock held out as well as in,
did he consider rituals, duties, days ahead,
did he say to them your best clothes are useless,
did he tell the first face I have missed you most?

HOME PRAYER

Good Lord, our shadow, be kind to Portsmouth,
and kind to the dead ones who labored there,
and kind to the Celias who buried them home,
and kind to teacher Willet we chased with liquor,
and kind to Mrs. Speers who fled from her dreams,
and kind to the winds that blew from our mouths,
and kind to the Elizabeth we fouled with our muck,
and kind to wallets in the Whitlow pockets,
and kind to Churchland's wharves where kinsmen went,
and kind to the lies the Navy made us market,
and kind to Gene Vincent singing on High Street,
and kind to black dirt that made us. Lord, admit
us, we lived here, almost happy, almost yours.

THE INNERNESS OF CHURCHLAND

Held up, fell down, I was little to gild.
Hurts, many. Scars, some. Which deaths sign you?
Jump back, jump back, jump. . . . Sins. I remember
New skirt, new place, new shirt, new boy, new man.
Am I? Where?
           What's called me? Can I go? Who says?
What number most masks us? We must begin again.
The next start of things in our mailbox. Good days
I played catch, played fumble, played pull her
Down with me, red-topped, God the father's honey.
Mother, what would you have me show or tell?
"Blood dripped, leg broke, a man died." I almost smell
Bridges Avenue, high leaves that hissed *Mine, child.*

HAMMER AND SICKLE

Where from? That noise that slid as if true
along the blue-gray stone, up hickory's back,
down ash, the clang-wang that tree-riding was two,
then shivered to many, spidered up a trunk
lit like lightning, big gleam and dribble's wash,
skidded slick from fist, so hard you heard, knew
by water's shudder what and where, below creek
waiting, it was: your father's straightening strike
down gouged sickle of steel; something in the grass
where he went, arms swinging, had bit at him, back
up-arm traveled, so to you, now, its passing
comes, his day-bruise, and years in age, memory's hook
makes him bend, blow. Sudden bang again, recoil's ring.

ELIZABETH RIVER WATER SKIERS

They towed us behind a white boat on this brown
skidding, this swaddling river of nouns in shit,
bubbled, clotting verbs loosed from suburb houses
where aproned war vets flipped their charcoaled meats.
Faces lifted serene to day's silent sun.
Why not? Hadn't they survived blown brains, blood bursts,
Japs, Germans, sea-sick speech, lonely holes with tits,
ticks, big yaps, that smell as cheap as a sweet walk
down Hatteras Beach? Now, at rivers, they lived
without asking too much. Let water thicken.
Let the self's slime, crusts, scabs, scummy gobs go
where currents want it to, where the center howls.
We'd whip by. Dads cooked, heads in smoke, burning words.

FIDDLERS

Black mudbank pushes them out like hotel fire.
Some at water's edge seem to wait for transport.
Others sweat, pale, scattered on the shining beach.
All keep closed the mighty arms of God's damage,
waving at shadows and movements made by the sun.
Desire, the dragging arm, sifts, picks, tastes, untastes
endlessly the civic occasions the tide brings in.
Surely floods, cold fronts, embolisms of dreams
drive them in where the earth's brain hums. They
clasp, breed. They glare upward in rooms where the moon
slips its question. Daylong they spout, fume, command.
Biblical as kinsmen with a son they must kill.
Nouns, verbs couple like years. Water comes, listens.

LATIN LESSON

Lank black hair to the doily collar at her neck, gray
streaks like road-snow, part hacked down middle,
Miss Roundtree, absolute as lightning's finger.
She'd watch the fields yield to new roofs, the highway
jammed by bulling trucks, lumber, glass, toilets, tar,
that path she'd cantered by creekside now a needle's
gleam past new bright steel, grocery store's marquee,
Casteen's shop closed, flies shooed, Bo's Do-nut's sandy
floors splintered, burned, and she walked cool as verb forms
stair-stepping in our heads when we clumped to school.
But what dead tongue did she give that I yet see swarms
of tears when I rise, bumbling through an ode by Horace,
her family man, who drank and never could leave home?

WRECK IN THE WOODS

Under that embrace of wild saplings held fast,
surrounded by troops of white mushrooms, by wrens
visiting like news-burdened ministers known
only to some dim life inside, this Model
A Ford like my grandfather's entered the earth.
What were fenders, hood, doors, no one washed, polished,
grazed with a tip of finger, or boyhood dream.
I stood where silky blue above went wind-rent,
pines, oaks, dogwood ticking, pushing as if grief
called families to see what none understood. What
plot of words, what heart-shudder of men, women
here ended so hard the green world must hide it?
Headlights, large, round. Two pieces of shattered glass.

A Lay of Spring

My father must have been cold in his casket,
ice slicking the bermuda lawns, roads, tulips
just trying to get born. I wanted him alive.
What could I know? I was sorry, seventeen,
not yet a man, brooding virgin, nonsmoker.
He left quick as his sizzled Pall Malls, wordless.
I kneeled with the heavy Baptists who prayed hard.
Then quiet, tulips came red, yellow, boozy sun
welding my eyes. The time I passed out was May.
This is my song. He's gone. I begged let me be
touched, for tomorrow I'll only grow older.
Alice fed me mountain oysters. Summer started.
Buds dropped. Alice swelled. Preaching? Poetry? You lose.

FIRST TOURNAMENT
LEARNING EXPERIENCE

You think you've got him figured, your dream drives bold,
slants of dusky light, winds, lay of land, sun-flamed
distances carried neat, the habitual stroke
with feet, hands, cock of chin all just so and, aimed,
you release the way the pro, deceased now, said:
covering the far flag, great shot; luck's good as dead.
But the little bastard shadowing you's stuck
close for nine, daffy chips, hundred-yard irons played
maddening as a boy with his dick, up, down, up,
down. On this par three, you've near knocked it in.
Then his scuffed wobbly crier dribbles up, drops,
a plop audible as halves of breaking wedge whiff
past unyielding oak, and memory's kiss, her handshake.

SELECTIVE SERVICE, 1965

Already silence rises into these mouths,
a thickness like blood cooling as the two move
around you, eyes like summer's butterfly here,
there, here, touching all the evidence you leave.
The leather glove soft, roofless rotted dog house,
yellowed rooms now dim. You've an arm patch you'll swear
leaped from the sleeve of campaigns no war remembers.
The Zippo with a man's red name and low flint
claps now and goes smokeless as weeds the wind's bent.
Thick male fingers fidget, slide, clamp, and untwist.
How can they recall the quick dream you made roar?
Who feels the cool magnificence of your town's dawn
before you'd turned and waved at the far edge of lawn?

IN THE NANSEMOND RIVER

A man comes to love the ground where he lives, yet
how does this begin, in what sun-varnished split
of time, what yellow leaf-fall, what graying scrape
rain drags along the dirt road? I cannot hope
to know who I am until I have learned what
all seems to know in unfailing flow: moment
by moment life is life, and death is more life.
The braiding wallside cries of cardinals climb
past where I lie, a boy, hoping I will go
far, trying to dream its shape, know what I'll know.
What day is it I feel my father's boat drift
slowly out, then back, caught in the tidal shift?
Pieces sail by, grass, paper, wood, frayed rope.

OLD COUNTRY

Why had nobody told me they'd be the words
I'd worked with since birth, and the mouth's makings
showed that flash of good teeth, that bloody tongue
all we could claim? Women so fair and upright
we made them angels in stories of killings
nobody could do as well as we had. The beards
our fathers wore surfaced among these and stunned
with thickness and length. Like crabs in the pot,
layered, making salute to death, they bubbled
and clacked and clung hard to each other's darkness.
I felt at home under the tall clock's rumble.
You had to look close to see how this business
meant to explode each sweet face and changeless heart.

BLOWFISH AND MUDTOAD

Held the wrong way either will take the finger
that clamps the casual pen, changing your words,
its rows of teeth like a serrated bread knife.
Moss-covered as bottom rock, wearing the brown
scum of salt water settlers, current-fluttered
flags of weed, eyes like glass pitted by age,
each reads steadily the downdrifted offerings
its tongue ticks for: crawlers, wings, limbs, all
the great current gathers to sweep away at last.
Our line sinkered into that steep wants a sleek
one to claim us—big Blue, Striper, Thor-like Drum.
Not these nibbling small-town preachers, Mudtoad's
black ambush, or Blowfish, resurrection and rage.

THE GODS IN MY BELLY LISTEN

Some nights the katydids cease, holding their breath,
gone still, and razzing racket of August heat
sinks inward like the insuck of air when love
lifts your face suddenly before mine. It gives
that shudder along the spine, the knife-through-meat
feeling you have when the doctor brings his touch.
Under long-armed black oaks and the pine's limp brush,
green lizards blow out pink macho throats, and wait.
Far off, blanched, glistening in this same moonlight,
swells slapping where the ocean seethes in distress,
something flays with long teeth a bloody other,
the small gust of lung's last comes, a heart flutters.
Stillness and fear walk inside me, night listening.

THE BULLPASTURE AND THE COWPASTURE COUPLE

The push and shove of two rivers at translucent
noose where pulse would get through, the pearly glister
of its birth so low on the register—who'd
hear? Softly Virginia's James summons and starts.
Red blurs from an egg shell, and now the first bird
Spring bleeds into the gray breaks loose, hunger's words
everything wants to speak. At the dead-end road's
end, water lies with whoosh and whip of first storm's
showering, its useless promise like our hopes
already running to silence, the blue place
no one enters while the tongue feels its harms.
B. B. King drifts through trees. Finch goes over,
someone lags in love. The sun's sax spooks its tune.

A SUPERNATURAL NARRATIVE

He wanted something to happen but it would not.
All day the cheep of cardinals over Spring grass,
lyric crows, raucous finch negotiations,
and yesterday the great owl's dire who-who. But
nothing happened; no one married, died, called
over the fence, ran off with a piece of trash,
tried to abort herself with a Coke, or swelled
at armpit with costs only the future knew.
Still, he thought, things must be happening, the blue
lights burned the ballfield, sirens spiraled, then hush
of machines from yard to yard, steady, and all
just life, what the moths ached for, the black widow.
Her web shook his room. He kneeled to get close.

SEAFARER

Look, he was writing, bemoaning his life locked
in days, years. All leaped like a love beyond him.
Then friends gave a gift, storm-tossed, once a fuel pod
from Navy jet, outriggered, now nimble, hipwide
boat for braving inner creeks. Sail unzippered,
he hiked each lip-swell, hiss heavy, safe and lost.
So sought he shelter with gladness, shy goings
out, waiting for tow-backs, his tacking one way.
Then friends hailed him: Sail-saddled walker of green,
why not play the blue deepest, past the calm point?
So he drove where no pine shades, saw unstopping
ambition's horizon. Then winds went. Exiled. Cried
"Rudderless, friends!" Seas blank as books at the end.

for Stephen Dunn

CIRCA 1650

Late afternoon's shifting clouds turn water dark
that sand in shallow scoops candles from below
like a book the fresh winds swirl. Reed-tips bend.
The air's palmful weight smells of foreign things,
hunger's gold bird flits coppery, quick as fish.
Surf piles harder on, its bubbles loosed, gone
the way you, grandfather ten generations back,
wake, walk soundless past cow and horse and head
of sleeping mother, who thinks the devil's night
ate and shat you off. Wind's cleaned the dirt's sign
you gouged for her, and rain at dawn. By dinner
you'd stand in surf's tug, watching water change.
The same for all of them, and me. That far dark.

A LIBRARIAN'S GIFT

How long had it lain there, coverless, red-back
spine spurning the midwestern dust like dignity
in faces that stand so before the plate-glass,
then shuffle wordless to the end of the street?
The librarian's hand in flared sun. *Your friend?*
Red Warren's selected. I hadn't read to the end
but did by dusk, rocking in shade. It was to me
the revelation, the gaze of Mary's that gasps
when the stone's touched. All since I can track
like the night spilling over asphalt, and dawn's
dew-glitter in yards I ran, and earlier mowed
for cash, needing my way in the world. But why
did that book rise just then? Like a face at dusk.

GREEN DUTY

Sitting in the sun I watch the cat chew
the head, then torso of a shy green lizard.
He rolls, soaks the day's heat, his meal
radiant as a good cigar in my uncle's mouth,
a man who died pissed at losing in Vietnam.
Near the lake's cove where the owl flares
its eerie call just to scare me midnights
when I am alone, writing, I saw a turtle
like a warped handball mashed into asphalt,
more image than flesh, yet with small legs.
I thought of my uncle, his big breath wheeze
when he crossed a road to cut mother's grass
because he loved her, and it was there like duty.

ELEGY FOR MY FRIEND'S SUIT

He saved all year for the gray suit, Brooks Brothers,
because he wanted the best, but left unworn
what the plastic shroud held. All night I watched, drank,
who outlived him by years. Tempted, I armed it.
Two blocks away surf rolled the ocean's good kiss.
He loved best a chance to ache for joy and shame.
The ball I went to slopped wet and raw. I stunk
up dawn, puddled the floor, a heap of seaweed.
His dead face cracks each time I ooze in the sun,
that squint he had from birth, no child's loveliness
in eyes that saw all. Women squirmed to touch him.
That kiss of death on his arm sighed "what a prick."
"But well-suited for dancing," he said, "if he was me."

NINE BALL

My anger's long for the room of broken chairs in rows,
spittoons with death's brown beauty breeding its glue
atop the stairs that clattered and turned you in
where they waited, shot, glared, and hooted, the goons
who knew more ways to make you "Rack and Pay" than
Pilate's birds in dusk's dark trees. I took my cue
hour by hour, learning what deceit is, the tuck, throw,
and cushion lean you'd need if they missed the break.
Near-sighted, I kept losing the paths they'd spun.
Then the shooters faded to just faces along the walls,
only tales in pieces, whispers. Then I bent alone.
They took all I had with a greased game of nine ball.
Come tomorrow, they said. I meant to. I still mean to.

WALKING THROUGH CAMOUFLAGE

First day of the world brightness, yet cold
that rinses all fears, shivers up narcissi,
trembles the lone-stalked rose, brings back
the dun cardinal, nest flecks in her clutch.
What is happening? The pond steams, loons
motor silently, buds like small heads appear
on each azalea, camellia, boxwood, and fruit.
Moving trucks grumble on the street, still
traffic's apocalyptic turbining reverberates
tree by tree, wall by wall, a flood of what?
Going where? Monarchs float, ignorant, under
the owl that woke us again at midnight, scar
on bark, unless you know where to look. I do.

II

A MAP OF YOUR SMALL TOWN

Sometimes there's nothing to write about, no news
the world wants to let go of, the sun held back,
answering machine aglow with its red emptiness,
even the house refusing its moonlight flash, its groan.
The cardinals and their babies flee deep in
some wooded otherwhere and traffic's taken a hike.
Mother said we'd need brass balls and sweet luck when
we found roaming what we did best, and dreaming.
Parked in the mental hospital's lot to talk,
we watched shadows move, dusk bled to black, and you
wanted to bolt like a shy horse, but no place
ahead called, secret, down roads you couldn't guess.
Joy flickered in lights on, off. Phones kept ringing.

Cows Calling

Some sounds have the heart's way in mind. They fit
what you're feeling, they're dressed up for a date.
You hear them in the backyard though distance
keeps them placed like joy beyond the meadows.
You might as well be dead as not to listen
when trains come roaring all excited about days
you haven't imagined yet. Even 18-wheelers say
a little something of the kiss like Spring mist,
and it'll waltz into your room as your pockets
spill on the chest whatever last glitter you have.
You add it up. Step outside. All those dark homes
wait with shirts, pants, combs. Their books fit you.
Don't the cows know that? What meter have they mastered?

GLENDALOUGH'S ROUND TOWER

Phallic, its speckled gray stone seems to leap up
in time mild as the valley road that uncoils
where the car park yawns with crowds. Dennis and I
dawdle, our wives snap photos of vaults as light
fails ahead. We stumble upon them, their lens set,
the Irish family on holiday: red-topped father,
now buzz-cut and ear-ringed, half punk, half Viking.
She's whipped, pale as ground flour, infant like a fruit
hung from her breast, five more shifting, hands clasped,
climbing to the slabbed stairstep. They grunt at stones
that pave the ground where western sun slices eyes
used to squinting. They want to play, the oldest
girl's frock lifting at gusts or the lad's first poke.

for Dennis O'Driscoll

BOYS IN THE SQUARE AT BOLOGNA

Across the courtyard of gold fountains at dusk
they strut, water lifting like smoke from penises
of stone. The dark earth cools as each one
preens in the square's mouth, indolents, masks,
beringed fingers, pigeons cooing for secrets
of the centuries oozed like spilled milk.
When girls come in silky heel clicks, three
whistle the air's exotic cries. They bob
like fish white for the moon. Some disrobe,
chests pale as panties, big neckchains, amulets
dancing, Marlboros, scooters' razz. The loudest
spout louder what fucking they will do tonight,
their hands miming the untouched and ripe.

GOLD BIRD AND THE AGE

Every gray day swells in around you, gold bird.
Sinister as the copperhead in thick russet
pinestraw, that held-back surge of piled up desire.
I think my hands were born to touch and weave with
air your intricate dips, veers, blinks always take.
I'm more than two of you, the juror sun quips.
Now my feet tap the lake route, saying "Where? Where?"
Should you fall for my gaze, I'd think of Groucho's
duck, before your time, that measly joke that's stiff
as luck, so all I'll ever taste is round zeros
of remorse, night's cramped pain. Still, if you were here
I'd offer you a drink, put on "Dancing in the Street,"
turn off the moon, be snakebit by dreamless sleep.

BREASTS

They nurtured the one who is sent away
for his bad dreams, for spinning toward desires.
They seized his fathers before him, and gave
what they hadn't known some were dying to offer.
There are none like yours. When I see you, from air
they seem to emerge, hover, and move on,
young, old, only women in supermarkets. But,
absent, yours still define you, like the stone
where you stood when you found them. It's been removed,
and the blank window you couldn't pass. Must you
be coupled and nameless, pinned to familiars
of your mother's shadow? Who are new women
scraped clean in their rooms, smooth as knives in water?

ONE WAY THROUGH OUR PUBLIC PARK

She was our school Queen, long legs in mini-skirt,
her girls gone, who takes the inner paths at fifty.
She walks hard, working off shadows. Her open
lips let teeth's dark show and tongue's liquid probe
seems grackle cry for words no one hears her speak.
The tale gives her a young man and soon they're pinned,
becoming two snakes raw-braided in Spring's garden.
What sad story's driven them to the dirt's place,
her silks pulled aside, their mouths locked into tastes
of all they've eaten, survived, and just keep down?
Long back we shivered on that cold bed of green.
She's my age still. When I pass this nightmare grove
I'll drive slower. You can't see much from the road.

LOUIS ARMSTRONG & THE ASTRONAUTS MEET AT THE LANGLEY AFB POOL

Eighteen, out to celebrate the fresh wedding
of his mother and the Major of Jets, he saw
the famous one wipe his brow and make the joke:
My Man Tan's sweatin' off! Brassy jazz rang.
The astronauts, brave daring doers, aped
whatever worst men can do. Drunk, howling, and raw
bodies moonsleeked, heads boiling in that quick blue
like planets, the swimming gods seemed telescoped.
He felt his youth, smoked, watched, was bound to earth.
The vision of great men shitting in the pool
blew something deep inside. They humped like goats.
With him, the girl he'd marry. Soon she'd fuck her boss.
While she puked, someone lifted the hem of her dress.

THE ENDLESS DAYS OF
SIXTIES SUNSHINE

Throbbing and gurgling, my engine might have been
the coveted Olds, chromed bald, Republican.
But I got my first ticket in a friend's Ford,
hot night, Elvis thumping hard. Born to Chevies,
tri-carbed V-eights, like hope's big dog loping off,
we vacuumed for scent. My chariot was gold,
same as evening sun that sent me for my baby.
We'd ride through valleys of years, Little Richard,
Sam Cooke rocking between her half-opened knees.
Passing town's bullet-dimpled sign, she made me squeal.
What arias with our kids. Then her tumor therapy.
Trust no old bastard, she'd shriek. That's how we lived.
Then we had war, dead President, dead King, no Beetles.

COMPOST PILE

When I told her the burial problem, what to do
with the dead dog that outweighs my old wife,
city ordinances against digging, lawyer's rules,
the cost of transformation of the past being dear,
she looked at me for the fool I've always been,
offered her compost pile, her awful wormy faith
in it, and must have seen pity's gaze smolder
across my cheeks, and guessed that inside I'd seen
a smokeless heat of decay that can eat a life
like battery acid on naked skin, desire flat
juiceless, winter-stiff, that growls but will not go.
She must have thought *I'll have to act the puppy part.*
Thus, she licked me in the dirt that stinks and steams.

OTTER LIKE A MUSE

Lithe as an otter, body of gold smoke, you
came where I was, romped with me, and did not leave
until our play turned too rough, like the age, then
teeth, muzzle's coil and snap, the slashed, parted skin,
blood's dapple on pond-face, cold deeps yielding.
We lifted from bottoms what time sifted down,
star-freckled ribs, live flesh we licked by streambank.
Any passing nudge of wind or last-gasp limbfall,
any nailed squirrel's digging all it took to
bounce us deep in. But skies betray us, winds spill
slabbed God-thought; rain skids, ice pulls me back
to dull of days living, flow's veer and spindle.
It won't be over. Pine's play shudders. You're all blue.

Answer to a Poet's Last Letter

The heat now's like that first night I taught you,
baking the broad-hearted sycamore leaves. Blear
haze too thick to see the James River's south shore
I hunted with grandfather, best friend, both dead
where pop shops, laundromats, drifts of trash shove
the few green farms left. We loved the unknown
advents of talk that drew us like hymns, the way new
poets scare themselves into lives made by work
not death's usual dreams, the cruel, stupid, or plain.
I watched you float toward home, that first steamy night,
plain dress, plain words. Your husband cried in the dark.
You asked why I wrote. I said lost things. This heat.
Sweat dripped. I'll be better soon, you said, you'll see.

CHRISTMAS LIGHTS STILL ON

Thunder's angry doorslam, then the papery white
flash like the inside of your thigh our first time.
It's so close the dog jams against my leg-back,
whoofs of wind bring a wave of water, so I
turn away, but not fast enough, the dribble on
my face like something's inside—as you were
once we'd met. It rained that night. At home
I thought sadness crawled out of dirt to howl,
as it would forever. I ate eggs and drank beer.
By Christmas you loved me. I danced and moaned
when cars left streets bare, or houses lay black.
When the storm shows my neighbor's Christmas lights
swaying, I watch for bulbs to burst, glass to fly.

FIELD DRESSING

No one ever forgets that ripe maggot smell
of entrails laid on your fingers, the blood-steam
rising to cling like weightless, sleet-bright seeds.
But here earth hides its usual electric, small
heart, lungs, liver refusing the stiffened host
whose eye, stunned, deflates like the broken air-sac
of the sister fucked under flies at a foreign wall.
No crop's touch and no planet-like gold pellets.
The bony foot, one spur, belies practiced heat
in your mistress, eating, her nipples like wing-nubs.
Remember your hooked nail worming where quail calls
start, the leached childhood field you longed to hunt?
Soft grass for bed, creamed skin, scented sweet cake.

WATERING THE DOG

Lying under the come and go of the storm
that's risen and harsh where lovers should steam,
it's hard not to think of days we charmed
sex like a dog to lie with us, whining
for more of whatever we had, a pocket
skin made so big we could hide in it.
What else leaves us sheet-wrapped, lapped
by all the breath a languid body has? When
out you tumble to shower off my stopped
heart's slack in its sack. Once we were young.
We coiled past time until our hides shone
red as if through the roof spilled the sun.
Now I hear rain gargle, the water on you sizzling.

ALMOST AT SEA

Morning light pours through our busted slats,
thick enough to float on it, a baby oil
whose scent is yesterday's Fritos and Coke.
It makes you sweat along the brow to wake here,
the air like a boat's bow upside down in May.
And yet faint like those fingers on your hips,
desire's nibbling so long known begins again.
Can you feel bobbing out-tides bump, crazy shrieks
from bombing birds that can't outfly their small lives?
I want to lie long where your legs drift apart,
listen to the freight's somber coming rumble,
feel the sun's buoyant resurrection slip
beneath us, lift us, and kiss the good years back.

THE LOUISIANA SEA OF FAITH

This land lies low toward the Gulf, a ridge
halved by the Mississippi, abandoned
where great sturgeon, shark, turtles cruised,
our daily rising mist the last letting go,
breath's rot fertile enough to root the lush
cycling of the short-lived and the hopeless.
Twice annually our people cry out and binge
for lives drained in the torque of a death
that clings like sodden summer shirts: Mardi Gras,
Christmas balance priests and bare-breasted women.
The winter sun yanks orchids from the darkness.
Men drift past the levee like beer cans, our mothers,
our daughters rasp "Throw me something, mister!"

STAINED GLASS AT
CHURCHLAND BAPTIST

Friends, we enter the sanctuary, a wedding's
beauty guiding us, in tall glass glow, the brass
dusklight hung below magnolias, oaks, pines. God
once growled here when we groped for holy presence,
shotgun boys scrimmaging shades. We bolted to cars,
dim rooms with dim girls, lies to mothers, our joke
the Baptist scream-and-thrash act. Preacher Moran,
bald as the moon, commanding as Milton's Lucifer,
broke storms of words to wash us of devouring sex.
Flesh peeled, brains boiled, scum-eyed, unless Jesus came
in us, we'd live untouched, swelling with our fears.
Like Mary, we giggled here. Today you lift the lace.
Chime slow your vows for what Mary's windows always kept.

for Edward and Cindy

46

ONION MOTHER

I can't help wanting to unpeel this mute hag.
Padding supermarket aisles in the latest hour
before closing, her finger drifts, bananas
brown, an apple infects whatever's near, flour
spills from a ripped box, bottles break. You can as easy
count on her paying pennies as the rain
when you have some stashed honey waiting. Tant pis.
Once coiled before a stage where I was speaking
she ate onions, groped a huge, clattery bag,
swung a half-mop, like an axe, at the usher,
a girl with nails like red moons. The crow purred.
She oozed on velvet seats. People saw the stains
love made with this wordless creature, farting happily.

THE FRANKLIN STREET QUADRILLES

Sun pours down on the quadrangle like gasoline
making its play the second after the match.
Love's teaching me new steps. A cat coils and whines.
I thank the blood-breech holly berry's red fetch,
the plump yellow petals urged from black dirt,
limp stems still too weak to hold a settling finch.
Why don't I know the names of all I survey?
The long blue silk of sky like her easy leg
lies down on my lap, late afternoon's just time
humming note by note a coed's dreamy shrug
at due dates for someone's touch. I watch one flame
her lips, stiffly sit to see who'll flirt.
Nipples quicken. Limbs weave, bow, and hardly touch.

WHERE THE GARDEN GROWS

They were married almost thirty years. He felt
the house shrink when she left for the weekend,
or thought he did. Absence was what he knew well.
She felt the wrath that set on him like a hurt head
because he was lonely. Or shouting. The devout
expressions between them, greased with wondrous tears,
accused and denied, swept, nosed like history
places and people they could no longer keep
in sight, like whoever lay in the coffin,
whoever walked the backyard beyond floodlights.
So she went to watch a group's huddled women
fret and sing. Then went home. He stood in rain's spit.
Night and day they found the odd, fresh smell of weeds.

OWL PLAY

Clenched to black oak's limb, no prospect visible, he
swivels, dreams out his flight, wings that drop him ways
nothing expects, yet all things know, along alleys
cat-footing close to walls, by ditch, under meazey,
grass-swoop sway of winds, the coming of pain. Please!
men mutter, and snarling dogs, flat on dirt, freeze.
He outlives gun-laden cokeheads, word storms, centuries
of steel's whistle, pushed by stone-gouging machines.
He hears hurtling star-hiss audible as the knees
a woman rubs, her late last bus going by.
In his cool nightroom he waits. Blinking his eyes,
soft tip-touch of feathers moon-grazed, bone pulleys
grind, God's engines whir. Mary's face, glassed, shines.

SITTING ON BABIES

The day I took your sister to college tears
bubbled from me in the parking lot like fear
in a woman at the cash register of
7-Eleven, stuttering gulps, breath's shove
hard under the breast where forever's mostly
trochees in a syntax like snakes. You ask why.
Because sunglasses and a gun at midnight
make long hours thump short, and infinitely sweet.
Words, too, recall the heart: the way you translate
"babysitting" for class makes me concentrate
on what poems do, and don't, and a girl rises
like dove cries in my mind, and the day's choices
seem like razors at my skin, or faith discovered.

for Catherine Smith

MAKING A STATEMENT

Thousands, lately, have asked me about my hair.
Why is it so long? Why haven't you cut it?
I think about Sampson, of course, and his woe.
His hair like thickets where I was born, swamps,
tall grasses bending with red-winged blackbirds
like a woman's nipples in the quick sun-gold.
I could tell about Sampson, about the girl,
but I say my head is cold. I need cover.
Playing tennis with a leggy blonde I love,
I admit I can't do anything with it, my youth.
She rolls her eyes into a smashing serve.
"You old guys," she sighs with her drop-shot.
Back and forth all day, yellow balls, long gray hair.

III

KEATS SPEAKS

Today I believe the world's wound's not the same
for those who bleed as for those who flee the blood.
Find it once pooling inside your shoes, pants, hose,
that smell contained by the closet where you hide,
glister on your fingertip like sudden flame—
a weight like the desert's breath seethes, burdens you.
Dogs sniff, drool when you pass. In dreams roaches brood.
Government spooks watch, the heart tears, panting days
no one knows where you're holed up. The girl's gone blue,
eyelids up, and gold as magnolia's first blossom
her eyes rot in your hold, plums in a hope chest.
When men bleed, someone sews it neat. Not the worst.
The seed washes out. What hands stink of is truth.

WOLVES

Hard to imagine they are there.
Wall-to-wall carpet makes hearing them
impossible almost and they get in
the door like mosquitoes and you don't
hear those long skinny legs and their
worn claws are flat like hooves
so they easily, quietly step over wood
planks or designer tile if you have that
and dark closets under the hanging
coats are good as thick pines to stand under.
That click, that snap what else, Farer, but
teeth, long and white as paper's agreement
they have come to make with you. Are you ready?

LUNCH

Hours of tapping keys and staring, sullen clouds
the morning's mood, all scud and bump, hold
and go, images of what's unknown, yet wanted
dissolving so the sun appears, the day yields.
The shade is cold but the courtyard's filled
with flume of light, the soul's warm surround
I bring my lunch to: Vienna bread homemade,
local cheese, its wedged hunks like marigolds
yellow and sharp, bologna's muscle added,
and mustard to make the eyes weep, and beer,
beaded Dutch, a fistful of chips, an orange
deftly sliced so, unbruised, inner light's let out.
Crows struggle with their rhymes. I eat, all ears.

READING FOR WILLIAM EVERSON

Cathedral arches over us, solid, the wood
California's forests yielded, festive glass
windows tall with spirits who'd loved us, and I
held the front pew with Levine and Kinnell, books
ready as swords, if we'd been mock king's guard.
Then you rumbled in, unannounced, among us.
Who'd ever seen anyone so leonine?
White beard untrimmed, snow-pack blue eyes, you spooked
three poets to stand stiff and silent and honored—
I saw Levine's shifting glance. Kinnell mumbled.
I stood as high as I could to say my words.
Books you'd written crooned in my head like creatures
trembling in your hands, as in your poems they'd played.

NATURE MOMENT

Dusk, when he walks, he asks himself *Is this it?*
Lake flat as rolled sheet steel, God's orange and purple
sky like a Cadillac never garaged, puffing
fumes still hung while the music maker's rolled on.
Fish boil up. The paper says they're distorted,
sores, too many fins, too few. He thinks *Evolution?*
Macadam hurts his feet, but doc warns the heart
needs rotation like his tires. The smashed turtle
asks his mom, years back, how to fix what's bleeding.
She turns then, like light from ligustrum's thick scent.
What was her smell? Kids rocket past, pealing laughs,
jittery last-minute finch calls from hairy darks.
Why make this turn? He knows bush, house, but not reason.

ON HIS SON'S NEW BLUE GUITAR

Genetic interruption, phase, interlude.
Metamorphic transit. In medias res.
He remembers *his* blue dome of possibles,
moonsleek pouring late nights, the dream's tight bedroom
wracked by that banging twang and chordal fizz,
the plugged-in juice of promise sticky on skin
no one saw, or guessed, as poetry's sequenced bite
note by note took up his ghosts. Himself he sold
old ways. Now this fungusy other's down stoop
whacking the bejesus from strings that won't break,
raftery racket he, once, thrummed to. Winds' wham
of shutter, roof's nail-rip, nightmare's whip to this
his prelude to eurekas for Walt, Ez, Tom, and Wallace.

ANOTHER NATURE MOMENT

My Deep South, still famous for heat, lassitude,
hospitality, and mannerly ways of
keeping its big gut-wrench with the past hidden,
unless you can read, or fail to see its trash
gets swept away one side of town, yet adorns
the other, is paralyzed. An invasion
of air tv claims from beyond our borders
spills its tingling brittle little mirrors all
over magnolia, azalea, marigold,
banana palm, hibiscus, and clinging rose.
Ladies step out, damage assessors, down flagstone
to lift shards of ice from dirt they've long curried.
They toss aside the dark face, still none they know.

DAILY MESSENGER

After tennis with Big Deal, the visiting poet,
sets halved, my slicing shots better for once,
and greasy burgers for which he offered up,
clouds swirl, gray scuds off like ship silhouettes
vacuuming distance; buttery sun pours out.
I drop off thirteen shirts, no starch please,
and find a man by the car, voice a low pout.
"Man," he says, "I got no bank. I got needs."
His shirt is polo, the little horse on left
tit a giveaway, his shoes pricey Nikes.
Suddenly I see my shirts hung, darkly wet,
as if I've died on the court, he's come for me.
He's black, in whites perfect for the tournament.

MISSISSIPPI RIVER BRIDGE

Running after dusk, I see the far southwest
corner of the lake shaken. Is it rising up?
Girders gleam in glaze of sun, the highest peak
wheels or feet can scroll over in this land,
no mountains, cliffs, gorges, wooded vistas,
little to make the heart thud for littleness
of man, except the slow clay-brown swell
the Mississippi drags past like hope, manly
water deeper than the bridge lifts in the air,
its movement hungry for our tossed nightmares.
We need crossing points to go, delighted as birds,
where all is down and swept under, but us, when
we grin toward snaky lights far off, still running.

FANTASTIC PELICANS ARRIVE

Gray wind across the lake's back comes raking,
tiny sails of white foam, crest after crest,
sun beating like neon against cold's slash,
solitary loon floating in the cove. Today
the good bankers, egrets and angular herons,
keep hours elsewhere, as if trouble is sure.
Yet clumped in a wide white pod that bobbles,
cell by cell seceding, swirling off, outspun
trajectory, coiling back like bad blues, pelicans
overnight have blown in, cranky songs, fat boys
seining the shallows for something not gray funk.
We runners stop, whisper. They float like joy,
sleek hens and gullet-swollen middle-aged monks.

Novelist with Harley

Black, liquid sound like earth screaming to burnout
showed us the bulbed tank squashed on a wasp's stinger,
heavy enough when it rolled it clung to you
like a drowning swimmer, but you sent it away,
sold it into Egypt, walked out alone in rain,
refused collect calls, retired with our failures.
We readers live it still. She hugs your waist, bright
hair sails. Then wires fused, a delicate graze
of leaves, and dust's impact like rain on Spring's roof.
Moralists in cells asked what blinded you, where
such madness meant to drive us all, but you froze
like heaven's mime, toothless, untongued, all there was.
They rolled you off, leaking. Sun swelled like snakebite.

ACCOUNTS

Unusual cold, wind rattles the palm trees, is this
the sound of death's morning air? Or guilt's?
Grass returns uneven, shade mottled, sickness
as on the downy forearms, the in-turning face
shadows prevent a lover's full knowing. Are you?—
the past lingers, damp, raw, chill, but a blue
space opens now and again. The telephone rings.
Names, future plots, endearments felt, half-said.
A cardinal, confused, bumps the window, sings
from plastic birdbath his joy, his love hidden.
Columns never add up, always too little, too much,
breath of the tax man faint, foul. Purple blush
sweetens at the fence. Today I come out ahead.

PERFORMING FICTION

I was asked to dine with a Turkish novelist,
a fine soft-shell crab, a yellowfin tuna,
exquisite red wine, and he told me why
in Ankara rarely rain falls, people die
a lot, his cat punishes him for traveling.
I'm poor, I think I may live in Ankara,
which I try to see with my eyes asquint,
watching him, translating thefts, like Robert Bly.
He has invented a wife with grim, sharp smile.
The audience he invents wants history,
but we read our fiction, he in Turk, me in me.
I am incoherent, sure, but perform well.
Silky blondes ask who we are. *Money,* we hiss.

WATER PITCHER

Alone, green, long spout, rubbery, plastic, the kind
stacked in tall edgy ranks in the Garden place
at K-Mart, set out for use, earthy in Spring.
They seem to say things need digging, get out pal.
They make you wonder what hand's been planning things.
Today my wife's placed hers to catch some rain,
though skies seem endless as the future of grass
that climbs on its own. Who says flowers need us?
It sits where the gutter's busted. Rain spills out
tapped deep it seems, better water that sprays
from her hand, love carted to what needs it most.
That I understand, my drinking in her years.
But what moon-surfing force pours the sun? What mind?

VELVET RUNNING

Camellias drop their gaudy silks like underwear,
the green so thick it emboldens wall-to-wall
everything we pass over, and lighter velvets
hang the slenderest saplings with an inner urge
like neon where the morning sun flirts with water
around our lake. The endless outcrying of birds
seems to heave a happiness they can't contain,
and I feel it, too, trotting through the checked
trains of azaleas in pink, white, a passionate
red that could be blood's seepage: a need stirs
in me to bolt with ordinary beauties on the brink
of dissolution, outrageously wearing the glows
our streets give up, parading, before limbs show.

WRECKAGE AT LAKE PONTCHARTRAIN

Baton Rouge to New Orleans, hauling Route 10,
workweek done, flying home with old tunes booming,
road jolts, shaken by the bodies revealed,
I come into the room of a long wood quiet
as a parlor. Wisps of moss like an elder's
beard. I fly by two snug grandmothers glancing
from a Chrysler. Miles on I'm shamed by the glare
of their pouchy lipsticked fear, a melted look
I see some dawns. Whose is the law of the eyes?
I turn loud Chuck Berry's "Go Johnny Go," pop
my beer, grin, alive. Then I slow down to watch
the insweeping lake, a carpet stinky, black,
giving under cranes who step ashore alone.

A GIFT FOR SEAMUS

1. FIRST MEETING, 1973

Snow drifted, a sky like raked sand, roads mute,
the yellow phosphorous glaze of parking lot globes
cast everywhere when I drove to hear you read
so far north I, too, felt "an uncertain paddy." Your words.
Southern, crude, inturned, I wanted then to heed
what others thought by hiding in poetry's crowd.
Cold enough to make the car wheels hum and ache.
Write about deep waters, you said, to Hammond's chords.
The flat's front throbbed with beery song, and in back
two bare babies slept, the heater holding out
ice and angry gripping cold. You understood
my love of crabs, fish, weird watermen whose names
clam rakes, empty pots, hooks, razored seasons maimed.

2. GROLIER'S, 1982

Louisa's book shop, wood floors, the scrape of my heels
raked through morning light, Grolier's poets. I stood
staring up at tallest shelves, head hurting, the night's
howl still on me, your *Wintering Out* in my fist,
clenched with others I could hardly afford. Failed
love slapped a woman, who stepped inside. I heard "You'll
miss me bad soon." Books throbbed with shaken wisdom.
She cowered in the room's far corner, and waited.
You watched. I was learning what I could take home.
I recall her smell, his meanness, fear's iron taste.
They'd stand alone while I walked to lunch with you.
You shoved at me Mandelstam's *Letters,* signed it
"Marie and Seamus—be true." We ate. Sweet December.

3. FLYING TO DUBLIN

Flying must make you wise, storms, in–out, time spent
as the Wandering Paddy, better than Santa's
navigations for gifts, and goaded by saints' books
you chastise us to stay put with what we love.
I love the sheer of wind, wood, wheels, whiskey, men
killing themselves for words. Many live with bliss,
boats, calm seas, lies swallowed to keep souls alive.
Earth's green and blue from planes makes me want to sing.
Our stewardess, bright as an apple, brings drink.
Soon your harbor rotates, small sails spool about.
I'm dreaming guns, tongues, sexy slow-spinning ambush.
An inner emigré. I'll wake in your perfect town.
Through rivering clouds, buckled, I start my descent.

4. Strand Road Meeting

So why are we alive? This feel for fleshworn weight
of tidal buoys, say, for oyster tongs, for water's black,
and pump's chilled steel you took the mouth's shape from,
a bow's sexy, naked flank, gives nothing to me
if not love's tale, the leaping hurt of buoyed halves
like spray, what's torn, split, bared, babbled in faith.
But understand? Sheer rattle of words, promise
of fair life through sweat, breath, death-gusts at glass,
our hearts iced as trout. The phone gave me the last
plea of the last kin I had. Then he was free.
I've cut at men with knives. Lied. My hand in flames
of desire sizzled like cheap meat. I've prayed
for deeps of water, still, grave, glare's aching calm.

5. LIFFEY

When first I heard this name, James Joyce spoke it, poet
singing that dire book *Ulysses*. His fine girl
sits on a rock, water pulls off her skirts, whirls
of sex in each wanderer's eye, hardly in hers.
She sees them pass up and down, the little hurts
of pride even a young goddess can't kiss off.
Kennelly said Dublin's not a town, much less
a village, more a series of encounters.
I face where Swift, Synge, Yeats fared green water's
outtide with the dreamer's tongue. Here cold winds boil
Dublin slops, cans, butts, rubbers. Joyce's bronzed steps
shine pub to pub, where hacks still hawk clanking verse
for pints, mums, sluts in black, our sad wayfaring souls.

6. VIKING SCRIBBLES

August. I watch the shipyard lights walk water
to Craney Island. My Dad's dead. Do spirits
walk like fireflies threading life in the weed-tips,
appearing though you've done no big deed? Vectors
of happiness, like age, come unasked. I slip
down paths I've seen among your garden's willful
rainbowed blooms, beauty's growth in Irish mists.
You stare at tides of stars, alone. I drink where
water's night moves rise, the swirls of memories
lives I can't let go or keep. Bushmills. Ice.
The Liffey made your blood, James made mine. I piss
in the river's moon where childhood's men yet dwell
in tales of better days. Then I grunt, zipping up.

7. THE GIFT

What could I give you back but slate-toppling waves
white-cropped now like you, wearing in and onward,
steady as the manhood of the heart? Friend, slaked
by dippers of words you've drawn for thirty years, I
find myself yet pulled by aching thirst for bursts
against the sunlit shore, that deeper black cold
welling up from somewhere bottomless like hurts
we've hidden under memory. You've the great feel
of things, broken faces, glint of what's best said
by gull-swoop, glance, the look down in that's a cry
unmade but by the delicate tongue of the gifted.
In me the chapped, sloshed underpool holds the sway
your singing makes, my gift to listen and to nod.

BRITTANY

I've set Molly's dish down, the oily scrimmage
of god knows what meat she loves mixed with kibble,
the way our kids fed her, when Dee comes banging.
The tale is quick: Molly's pointed, flushed, mouthed
a finch she carries like an egg into darkness
of magnolia and camellia, no easing her out.
Barefooted, I stand in grass and watch, silent.
I'd like to say a father knows why she'll come,
as soon she does, dropping her prize in my palm.
A little lathered, but safe, this new flier
rolls, wobbles, then lifts to a dogwood's first limb
that springs, the way Molly does, in the genes' urge
to be praised for catching life, and giving it up.

IV

ARCHITECT

I never pretended people must be happy.
Should they live as they do? Let's put it that way.
Problems with heat, cold, open space, closed space,
lack of air, customers thought me imprecise.
Forever begging for changes. I gave them debt
they couldn't hope to repay, lifelong ache, guilt.
They praised me. I said I am what I am, what I build.
I had to leave. How could they forgive me, pray
as they might? I held back, shadowing myself.
I took what they offered as if it were proof
we had futures together. Who scammed who, plans
forming in their minds, bubbles on scummed streams?
Your place or mine? I like to joke. They make me.

ABOUT THE FARMER'S DAUGHTER

Under the oily willow on that scrub farm
the woman swung the white chicken. White feathers
whoofed and whiffled like a small February storm.
Years later he would see the pearls of blood spit
bright on her puffing cheeks. Then saw lathered
the beak of the bird, its pried wedge of darkness.
He stood in that thicket wary as a warbler,
unknown as her anger, as if he'd been Jesus,
and he wasn't, only one she'd said yes to,
when he asked what he'd asked. Yes, and skin ripped,
she said yes, some kind of weird spin in her chest.
When he'd hear that thump-thump like feet on porches,
he'd think how she smiled, shy, somebody's daughter.

ONE HUNDRED TWENTY-NINE DOLLARS

The law says you can dig the hole or buy it.
July, heat same as Louisiana's usual barbecue,
I take the axe to chop my boxer deeply in
and whack and whack and whack three clay inches,
an hour's sod, task for eight hours I calculate,
wheezing, sweating like an emphysemic. Crowns
of dust rise on weed-leaves, a golden nimbus
I must be smoking as I hack, chip, and gouge
what God's word says we'll all end up in.
The bloated body, wrapped in his old rug, waits
as always when I stop, black eyes wide, watching.
The vet's hole costs $1 per pound, so I pay.
Fouled, barked over, the room of the world stinks.

AUDUBON AND CHA CHA

Bent, opened, on my back for the new hygienist,
watching Audubon's brown pelican, its gaze
startled as if she's recognized me—why
do I think it looks obsessed? "I'm Cha Cha," say
plump hands in my mouth already digging down
where the days have weakened my stiffest root.
She pushes as if in desire, her blade scrapes.
Half-moon earrings chime against my cheek.
"So what's on your mind?" I'm gagged, I see those
shadows the bird eyeballs, a day bright as a tooth,
not breath sweetly foul, not pain making rooms twist
as my blood runs. Her breasts float like lilies.
Praise Audubon. Praise pain. Praise Cha Cha today.

DOCTOR'S OFFICE

There's never anything good to read is there?
Only plenty of the dated stuff, like deaths,
the usual missing page of *Field and Stream,*
its multi-color ads for bullets guns ruffed
grouse; also *House Beautiful,* foyer, parlor,
wings rooms like nobody's home we know cheesecake
so good-looking seas will scab before any's
on your plate; last year's *Time*'s Man of the Year,
the crisis still unsolved, the parent rag
no one reads, same place same people same movie
review, and who's the sick person sits down and asks
what's your pleasure? Nurse like the muse says you can go
in please your balls aching. Thanks. And no escape.

OLD FRIEND

Tortured, killed, MIA? I recall you gentle
in years of teenage aches, giggles, wrong turns.
Now your letter spills the words I can't hold
when I lift them again and again: two tours
in Vietnam, the MIG beaten, Top Gun School.
You've become the warrior I wanted to be,
and four fine children to host a coming age
of real tall tales with fists of good booze.
When did we meet last? Before my college rage
swarmed me to marches, placards. Who rules?
I enlisted to escape, my adding machine
quick, angry those four years I did. We're old
uniforms now. Life sucks. Who among us wasn't fooled?

THE RIGHTEOUSNESS OF FARRAKHAN

He's been to the doctor, an ailing right eye,
grit in it, maybe, a shape odd as a man
that floats back everytime he blinks, ragged
outline, and a haze always like a field fog.
No memory of what happened or where can
be dredged from his brain's deep-silted bottom,
yet anger sucks at his ankles like a slough,
walls rise against him, a bush barks like a dog.
Brothers sustain his lookout; nothing blinds them.
He feels the fury of the pure, focused now.
His one side is clearer than ever, a Jew's
glance all he needs to know what's in the street.
He can shoot low, if he needs. Healing can wait.

What I Got

Drillers, cutters, pliers, all rust-puckered,
three lawnmowers, sputterers, inherited
Zurich White, Spruce Green, Lipstick Pink, cans
it's anybody's guess what room, nails, bricks,
four coiled electric cords, taped, drawers of all
the on-off gone bad switches, wires, plugs, years
living with memory's dead makes me keeper to.
Things to scrape, bang, drill, saw, and sizzle,
not to mention boxes of notes, bills, photos
from sexy jaunts, diners, motels forgotten.
Touch a thing, you wonder if they named some name,
if they grinned, jerked hand back, or plugged it in.
This stuff owns me, piled, layered. Like all wisdom.

PALM TREES AT
1430 KNOLLWOOD DRIVE

Yul Brynner might make an entrance under them, brass
breastplate flashing, that famous skull nicely soft
where fronds wash the humid air for hard-eyed folk.
They're regal as deacons on the Baptist steps of
resurrection day with the light pink, unwicked
for once, the other trees in greenest essence
as befits a chorus, a cardinal's flame trumpet
surging precisely in domestic suites of notes.
For years I've moaned I can't write God's poems
but now I see the sentry palms laugh like men,
and each rattles a single fist of annual fruit,
small and dark gold, an emblem hissing *Praise me!*
In brief bursts everything does, this Easter Sunday.

THE COLLAPSING LIBRARY

Sun jams the rooms, heats the air, shoulders past
floor-to-ceiling books bloated with a language
you might call love's once you'd become a poet,
strophe after strophe taking up the least space,
mice leaving little turds behind them, silverfish
snoozing like whiskered dreamers as they vent
their paper-filled bellies, their ink-swelled veins.
The weight of the inner world is turning
up in tiny knots these creatures ingest and set
exploding in sun-puffs, spores we spurn, sneeze,
and suck in while the tv drones its game.
What makes us burden ourselves with abstracts?
Poetry's killing me, this death of hungers and shit.

REMEMBERING CIGARETTES

Kirk Douglas plays a sleaze in this matinee,
Sunday, me sprawled on the couch, feeling fey
the way more and more it happens, everywhere
wicked sun dripping down on finch wing, the fire
like blood's backbeat. It makes him stroke a match
across the typewriter's stilled carriage, the hatched
spurt in his carved cheeks a man's hook, appetite
gnawing inside for and against what? Hot, tight,
he turns back into black and white unreeling
that never stops, somebody near him steely
with youth's cramp from eagerness to get up, on
toward night's faster action. Soon he'll lie down.
But now smoke he's holding drifts out good, slow, steady.

TRAIN TO ST. ANDREWS, SCOTLAND

Not like Italian trains, raucous joy, crowds,
rows with students stealing seats, loud music
with tickets waved, conductors' sweaty grins, Huns,
Frogs, God knows what, and the wish for English words
the same old outsider ache when fine villas
loomed, anger's slow boil at boss's *Comprendo?*
Now lingo grunted *mine,* kelp-green fields ticked
with mists, gusts drove at seas two red-haired girls
on bikes bobbing a broken road. White house smoke
locked down villages, water's cold face like fjords
where kin once hid in trees. Then too dark to see.
I got off last, in wind. "Smith?" my contact wailed.
Whiskey, fire. Dawn-frost, the train's shuddering lyric.

for Douglas Dunn

IRISH WHISKEY IN THE BACKYARD

Two dwarf oranges, one tangerine, one grapefruit,
rescued from K-Mart's clearance sale, leafless souls,
luminous with Louisiana sun, volts
near liquid, rare buds of white like a woman's part,
the green waxy leaves it takes a long time to
open to peak conception, which is work, fate,
or luck good as orphans get. December's blush
here might be Christ's happy gaze spilled, not salt
lapping every road you take, not cold house-ache,
not winter's bloodless shuffle past dark and light,
faces like roadside toads, flashbulbed and stunned. But
who knows what happiness is? I drink and stroll,
Lord. Night comes cool as years ahead in clamped vaults.

THE PENUMBRAL LEGACY
OF HUEY P. LONG

There's an election here every week. Life's costly.
The boys stand for judge, commissioner, or school board.
We give them sweet syllabic schoolyard filth to hurl
if you're brave or fool enough to walk our streets.
Years back we tossed rocks. Now it's automatics.
We're enswirled by Nike Airs, Polo running suits;
gold chains orbit our necks; we could easily be kings.
We're impressed by all that you don't have, kicked back
when girlfriends split, burdened by work that stinks.
We'll vote ourselves big dicks, fast cars, no dying.
We'll drop your blossom-buried back fence like pants.
You'll be sore piles. We'll throw things out and grow.
We've got votes enough to keep things changing our way.

FIREFLIES AT BENNINGTON, JULY 4

Do you remember? The town flagged at twilight's flare,
banked coals, somewhere cabbage coiling about,
unknown meat, Sunday, maybe the first tufts of
green in sidelot shadows. Well, like that.
John's wife was whole and he had the rockets,
wonderful moustache, gin fizzes, elegant
tales he would write better in travel books,
such laughter you'd have thought the judgment day
come, gone, and us the winners, so much love—
but, of course, it was going to change. Cooked,
that's how we felt in early heat waves, and fat,
and old, too, and the icy stream made us shout
when we swam, though she didn't, she only stared.

QUAIL

Recalling old hunts, we rake ourselves with hooks
of briars along the bottom where a dog's stiff.
Field seeds fleck our cracking lips like blood, mouths
moving every step, taking sky, limbs, and weir
birds break from all at once. One won't come out.
It stamps and clucks and waits in death's little room.
"Bit by bit the world falls away." I hear your poems.
But what part's ours, I think, my grandfather's gun
first time in my hands? It slams me back, half-squeezed
when stinkbirds skitter. Tired, we chatter, pained
by having knocked from air just words, and now gloom
makes us kick the dark-gathered bush, then harder.
To make the dog stay, we coo and chime "Whoa, dead here."

for Charles Wright

BURGLAR ALARM

That wee-oop wail in the night's boggy middle
can wake me like stones flung on a tin roof, but
I'm already awake, outside by the brick wall
when it goes off, so startled it feels inside me.
The cramp comes, then, bending the body double
just an instant before you sprint. The distance
you need's never clear. You might not get away
despite repenting, prayer, gifts to good causes,
forgiving hugs by those who own the bullets
of innocence. Years pass in backyard instants
like trembling synagogues, or lumbering bees.
I peek over the wall to see what trouble
means to assault me now, careful, toes feeling the dirt.

A Tune for Maura Dooley

Who are they over there? Where do they get guns?
Imagine how they've gathered: Mom, Dad, Sis, and
Sis, late dinner and then the telly. Do they
do things like us? A glance between the sitcoms,
wine's little blood on Mom's lip and napkin.
Dad's funny swirl of hair where his cap's been on
from work, and the good, latest news has been said,
when they roar. Think of that, friends, as we spend our
lovely cash. We don't know them, not a one, or
what their weekend was, or what dream vacation
they'd leap to name if chance invited. Worlds away,
the dead don't speak of us, as we wish. Think how
cold technology's left them. Like spaghetti.

GHOST HOUSES

In Sudan there are houses for beatings, unmarked
residences in bright pastels, colonial maybe
in style, porticoes with wide-armed fans, ferns,
thick buzz of summer flies, and down the walk
the cry of a child fallen, close streets, engines
motoring afternoon passengers reading the *Times*.
Without numbers, no mail comes, no neighbors.
No teenage music seeps under doors, no cats purr
for a tossed scrap, no telephone rings on and on.
Anyone could slip in to spend the night, windows
unlocked, doors ajar, all dogs long taken away.
Imagine the black limousine that might bring you,
ceremonies when they greet you, your brave words.

A DODGE MAN WITH NO DAUGHTERS

Awful, the wordless splatter of thump and tinkle
I learned when a man drove his Dodge into dogwood,
and I leaped through my screen door, the first one there
to find him sprawled like a tulip cut down neat.
He looked like me. His nose ran and lips quivered.
His dim yellow teeth bit the air. Liver spots,
like futures dreamed, the brown on hands, on forehead.
Still as the undead, he slumped on bloodless seat.
A monarch blew in, checked him out, saw he was old,
oozing, not necessary, and swooped quickly
through summer's other days. He raised himself then,
kissed his wife, saw how he lived, hit the gas again.
A man's just noise without daughters, a wife, and a tree.

CRYING IN THE STREETS

Self-hatred waits on us like the garbageman
splattered by our family's week of smells,
ready to leap down and swing and throw up
the pushed-in, packed, ballooning litters we
are unwilling to keep longer. His smile seethes
malice and love of this work. He takes truths
home free for the lifting, beauties we miss.
When he cries out in the street to stop the truck
that's wheezing and banging like history, our hearts
panic like pigeons. His motions, smooth as chess,
work each neighborhood; he's learned to be discreet.
If you speak, he will turn away, or merely nod,
taking up our worst secrets, more punctual than God.

STALLED ON THE EBB TIDE

Out against the darkness, against absence, strokes
glowing in what is not light, exactly, plank
by plank we push ahead into freshets and shudders
of water, black time glinting. The boat rocks
but holds, for now, what we put into it,
flesh, blood, the smell of sex. How did we become
what water wanted more than earth? We are dregs
of things, last flickers bobbing, out of the fire
of the sun floating the good days, unclaimed,
as pure as seaweed. If we cry to the stars,
thrown free of waves, what hope thin as finned crusts,
belly up, ichthyan, can beach us in night's small skiff?
Piece and piece and piece going by. Moonstuffs.

CANARY WEATHER IN VIRGINIA

It comes in sharp, salt smell above James River's foam.
It clatters past azalea, willow, the exhumed sway
Of laurel, camellia's pink-smoked buds dawning open,
Oiling a woman's hands to spill moonlight in woe's rooms.
It flings unseen to any where he lives bands of wind
Unfolding so many gold birds dawn sings with god-breath.
Yellow-red streaks pass like her hair over his pillow.
What mission has it in droughty fields, uncoiling faith
That remembers to bring also cardinals, owls, gulls?
Swamp-sheen, a dew-gilt mast, mullet leap, cold horse-eye
Lift, hold him up, though he stiffens, alone in his yard.
When tides wash distance in, he floats, fate's kite, back
To silhouettes of pine, boats, the whirling yellow birds.

DESCENDING

Remember that tin-foil day at the beach descending
on water the color of slate, the man descending,
just a bald head like an emptied melon descending
God knows where, same day a shy girl-child descending
with doll and bike to darkness where, descending
the hill with dumptruck vizer down, sun descending,
a father squints just once and the years descending
ever now spin him like a pump's flush-pipe descending
to pure waters he can never reach and, descending,
what of wings flamed gold, dusk's holy glow descending,
heron, tattered, wearied, news-heavy head descending,
that's left by hunters to float all night, descending
as they do into sleep, the earth clean, just descending?
Where, and with whom, are those we've seen descending?